The Day the Circus Came to Town

The Day the

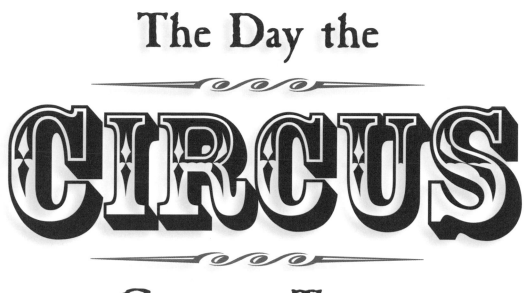

CIRCUS

Came to Town

Melody Carlson

Illustrations by Ned Butterfield

Crossway Books . Wheaton, Illinois

A DIVISION OF GOOD NEWS PUBLISHERS

The Day the Circus Came to Town

Text copyright © 2000 by Melody Carlson

Illustrations copyright © 2000 by Ned Butterfield

Published by Crossway Books
      a division of Good News Publishers
      1300 Crescent Street
      Wheaton, Illinois 60187

Art direction/Design: Cindy Kiple

First printing 2000

Printed in the United States of America

LIBRARY OF CONGRESS CATALOGING-IN-PUBLICATION DATA
Carlson, Melody.
   The day the circus came to town / written by Melody Carlson ;
illustrated by Ned Butterfield.
      p.   cm.
   Summary: After other boys ridicule the idea of going to the circus,
Billy almost passes up the chance to see one for the first time.
    ISBN 1-58134-158-X (hc : alk. paper)
   [1. Circus—Fiction. 2. Peer pressure—Fiction.] I. Butterfield, Ned, ill.
II. Title.
PZ7.C16637 Day 2000
[E]—dc21   99-086595
                                            CIP

15	14	13	12	11	10	09	08	07	06	05	04	03	02	01	00
15	14	13	12	11	10	9	8	7	6	4	4	3	2	1	

To Pamela Baker
(a good friend over the years)

with love, Melody

▽▽▽▽▽▽▽▽▽▽▽▽▽▽▽▽▽▽▽▽▽▽

Slow down, son!" called Mama as Billy gulped his last spoonful of soup and leaped from his chair faster than a fox out of a hen house.

"Gotta go, Mama," called Billy. "I finished my Saturday chores, and now I need to meet Seth and the fellas for a game of stickball."

"Don't forget about the circus, Billy," warned his little sister Emma. "Remember, Pa is taking us all to see the circus tonight!"

Billy paused for a moment as he pulled his cap down over his brow. He'd never seen a circus before and didn't rightly know what one was. But it must be special because everybody in town was talking about it. "Don't worry, I'll be back in time," he yelled as he shot out the door.

The boys played stickball all afternoon, laughing and shouting as they took turns at bat. Back and forth they raced across the hard-packed dirt of Main Street, stopping only long enough to let an occasional wagon pass by. And now it was Seth's turn to bat again. Although Mr. O'Malley had warned him time and again not to hit the ball near the store, Seth smacked the ball right through the open door of Mr. O'Malley's Mercantile. Billy watched with wide eyes as the ball knocked into a neat stack of tin pails, making them clatter to the floor. In the next moment the angry storekeeper burst out through the door with the hard rubber ball in his hand.

"You rascals, get over here! I'll take care of you once and for all!"

"Gotta go!" yelled Seth. "I hear my Ma calling." He darted down the nearby alley with his friends right on his heels. Billy was scared. He knew Mr. O'Malley didn't like kids. What would the old man do if he got his hands on them?

"Whew, that was close!" gasped Seth as the boys paused in the shadows to catch their breath. Billy's knees felt like wet noodles as the four of them slowly backed up onto another side street. Then just as Seth peeked around the corner for Mr. O'Malley, Billy bumped into someone directly behind him! He jerked around, bracing himself for Mr. O'Malley's angry voice.

But Billy nearly leaped out of his socks when he laid eyes on the weirdest-looking stranger he'd ever seen! Right there before him stood a man dressed in wild clothes. His orange hair stood out like brushed sheep's wool, and his big, red nose in the center of his painted face looked a lot like the rubber ball that had just knocked over Mr. O'Malley's pails.

"Seth," warned Billy in a quavering voice. "Hey, you guys. Look at—"

But Seth was already sizing up this odd-looking man. "What in the world are you?" he demanded in his toughest voice.

Seth was the bravest boy in town, and at that moment Billy admired him more than ever!

ello there, boys! I'm Zino the Clown, and I want to personally invite you to Pepperotti's World Famous Circus." The clown smiled and held out four colorful tickets. Billy reached for a ticket. If the circus was anything like this Zino person, it must be a whole lot of fun!

"No way!" declared Seth loudly. "I ain't going to no sissy circus. I heard all about them circuses. They're just for babies and wimps and churchgoers and the like." Samuel and Jack followed Seth's lead, and they refused Zino's tickets too.

"Well, how about you?" Zino turned his attention to Billy.

Billy's hand was still out, ready to take a ticket. He really wanted that ticket, but then he saw Seth and the other boys scowl at him. "No thanks," he muttered, his face hot with embarrassment. "Circuses are for sissies."

What a joke!" laughed Seth as he jumped onto a fence and began to walk across the top rail. "That stupid ol' clown thought we'd go to a circus! Ha-ha! What's he take us for anyway— a bunch of country bumpkins?" Seth jumped down and playfully punched Billy in the arm.

"Yeah," agreed Jack. "That Zino probably thought we were just a bunch of dummies." And the more they laughed and joked, the sillier the circus seemed, even to Billy.

"Well, you'll never catch me at no sissy circus!" yelled Seth as he waved good-bye.

"Yeah," called Billy as he turned toward home. "Circuses are for sissies!"

illy got home in time for dinner, but there was no dinner cooking. Instead, he saw his family all dressed up in their very best Sunday-go-to-meeting clothes.

"Billy, did you forget that we're going to the circus tonight?" exclaimed Emma. "Pa's got four tickets!" Her blue eyes sparkled with excitement.

"I ain't going to no silly circus," boasted Billy, trying to sound tough like Seth. "Circuses are for sissies."

Emma's smile vanished. "Is that right, Pa?" she asked. "Are circuses for sissies?"

Pa laughed. "Well, I'm no sissy, Emma, and I'm going." He turned to Billy. "Guess I won't make you go, son, seeing how you got your mind all made up. But your reasoning does sound a bit foolish if you ask me. Especially when you've never even been to a circus."

Mama just frowned as she tied her bonnet. "I sure do wish you'd change your mind, Billy."

But he just shook his head. "I'm not going, not now, not ever!"

"I hope you're not sorry, Billy," called Pa as they headed out the door.

Billy stood on the porch and watched his family leave. The truth was, part of Billy *did* want to go to the circus with his family, but Seth's harsh words still rang in his ears. And more than anything, he didn't want Seth thinking that he was a sissy.

"Don't be silly," he told himself out loud. "Circuses are just for sissies!" Then he decided to go find Seth, Jack, and Samuel. Together they'd laugh their heads off about how that clown had tricked those poor, dumb folks into going to that sissy circus.

But the streets were strangely empty. And when Billy knocked on Seth's door, no one answered. When Billy walked through town, no one was there. Had everyone gone to the circus? A bright-colored poster blew across the boardwalk and landed across the top of his boot. He picked it up and read, "Pepperotti's World Famous Circus. Saturday Night at 7 P.M., Bailey's Field." *Well*, he thought, *maybe I'll just head over that way, not to go in, but just to see what this silliness is all about.*

As Billy drew near Bailey's Field, lively notes of happy music filled the evening air, and in the distance he saw colorful lights glowing cheerfully in the twilight. He began to walk faster, his heart racing with excitement. Maybe he'd been all wrong about the circus! And then as he came up over the rise, *he saw it!* Like nothing he'd ever seen before—right in the middle of Farmer Bailey's cow pasture sat an enormous tent, bigger than ten barns all put together and striped with all the colors of the rainbow! Hundreds of lanterns lit up the whole area, and flags and banners waved in the evening breeze. So, this was a circus! Why, it looked fantastic!

Billy ran all the way to the entrance of the huge tent and peered in. To his surprise, he spotted Jack and Samuel just taking their seats—the very same boys who had agreed not to go to any silly, sissy circus! Billy started to step inside too—

old it right there, young feller," rumbled a deep voice. Billy turned and stared up into the face of the biggest, strongest man he'd ever seen. The man wore a suit of animal fur, with big leather bands around his thick wrists. "Ticket please," boomed the deep voice, not in an unfriendly way, just powerful.

"I-uh-I don't have a ticket," blurted Billy. "You see, I-uh-my family is in there and my friends and—"

"Sorry, son. No ticket—no circus." And while the man looked truly sorry, he still didn't budge from his post, blocking the entrance. So Billy turned and walked sadly away, back into the shadows, back outside of the big, bright tent. From there he heard the crowd clap and cheer and the music playing merrily.

e thought of his family inside the tent, enjoying the circus together. Oh, why hadn't he listened to them? And then he thought about Seth. What a fool he'd been to take Seth's word about the circus! What did Seth know about circuses anyway? Suddenly Billy realized that he should have done his own thinking. *But now it was too late.*

Billy sat down on an old stump and buried his head in his hands. He knew it was a sissy thing to cry, but the lump in his throat felt bigger than a watermelon in August, and he just couldn't help it. He wiped his nose and looked longingly toward the colorful tent. He'd never seen anything like this in all his born days! Nothing like this had ever come to Crocker's Grove before. Probably never would again either. . . .

Just then he felt a gentle hand upon his shoulder.

He looked up to see that strange clown gazing down at him. "Did you change your mind?" asked Zino kindly.

"Yeah," sniffed Billy. "I was sure stupid not to take that ticket. I never should've listened to Seth. You know, those other boys are in there right now, probably having the time of their lives too!" Suddenly he remembered the tickets in Zino's pocket.

"Say, Zino, have you got any more of those tickets? I mean, if your offer's still good, I'd sure love to see the circus!"

"Sorry, son. I gave them all away."

Billy's heart sank lower than a gopher on a rainy day. "Figures," he muttered. "Just my luck." He slowly stood, ready to go home. Sitting on the outside of the circus wasn't much fun.

"But," said Zino with a warm twinkle in his eye, "let's see what we can do." Then he took Billy by the hand. Now Billy felt a bit foolish holding hands, especially with a clown, but he didn't let on. Instead he just walked with Zino toward the entrance, wondering what a funny old clown could possibly do to get someone into the circus with no ticket.

"Evening, sir," said the big-muscled man with a polite bow.

"Good evening, Chester," replied Zino.

And then he led Billy right past the big man and straight through the entrance with no problem at all. Once inside the big tent, Billy found music and color and lights—almost too wonderful to take in! And as they walked, he spotted great big elephants and high-stepping horses; there were dancing bears and trained lions. And all around him were people in beautiful glittering costumes, doing all kinds of impossible things. Billy stood and stared at the sights in utter amazement. It was like a fantastic dream, almost too good to be true! And to think, *he'd almost missed out on all this.*

They continued to walk along next to the front row, and suddenly Billy noticed how all the circus performers waved and tipped their hats to the clown. And just then Zino stepped right into a finely decorated box seat and sat down in a big red velvet chair. Why, it looked just like a king's throne! And then Billy saw the name carved there—Zino Pepperotti! That funny clown who had offered the free tickets in the alley actually owned this entire circus!

Zino pointed to the seat next to him. "Would you like to sit with me, Billy?" With wide eyes Billy nodded. Why, this was the very best seat in the whole circus!

"Thanks a lot, Zino—I mean, Mr. Pepperotti," said Billy with respect.

"You're most welcome, son. But just think, Billy, you came this close—" Zino held his fingers just a hair's width apart. "—to missing out."

Billy nodded quietly. "I know that now. I can see how foolish I was to let my friends do my thinking for me. And it's too bad Seth is missing all this."

Zino nodded grimly. "It's a shame; I had hoped he'd change his mind."

"Well, I'm sure glad I changed my mind!" exclaimed Billy as he joyfully looked around at the happy people filling the stands. He even waved at his family just a few rows away. Then he turned back to Zino. "And I'm sure glad you gave me a second chance. Thank you so much!"

Zino smiled happily. "And I'm sure glad you came, Billy!"